Epic Poems for Epic Kids

Rachel Bishop

BookLeaf
Publishing

India | USA | UK

Presentation by *BookLeaf Publishing*

Web: www.bookleafpub.com

E-mail: info@bookleafpub.com

ISBN: 978-93-5744-958-8

First edition 2022

DEDICATION

For my children, Toby and Phoebe -

Thank you for always being my inspiration

and for teaching me that age doesn't matter

unless you're a cheese or a wine.

Dave

At the bottom of my garden,
Lives a peculiar elf.
He never says hello to me,
He lives by himself.

I see him hang out his clothes,
On a thin washing line.
Tacked to his door,
There's a 'DO NOT ENTER' sign.

He lives in a mushroom house,
Bright red and white.
It's not very large in size,
Not even knee height.

I wonder if he's lonely,
I thought in bed one night.
He doesn't have any friends,
Or family in sight.

The next day I visited,
That peculiar little elf.
I posted him a letter,
And introduced myself.

A few days went by,
And I hadn't heard a thing.
So I left him some cookies,
By the old tyre swing.

Each time I went to visit,
I'd leave a little treat.
Until one day there was a note,
Asking if I'd like to meet.

I made a little picnic,
And waited by his front gates.
We sat and ate together,
Now the elf and I are mates.

He still doesn't talk a lot,
But he always gives a wave.
At the bottom of my garden,
Lives my peculiar friend Dave.

What Will I See?

I'm walking through the jungle,
What will I see?
There's a sleepy, snoozy sloth,
Hanging out in a tree.

I'm walking through the desert,
What will I discover?
A sandy camel calf,
Walking next to its mother.

I'm walking through the Antarctic,
Who lives here?
A grand emperor penguin,
Belly sliding with no fear.

I'm walking through the mountains,
Who's over there?
A goat with curly, black horns,
Climbing rocks without a care.

I'm walking through the Arctic,
Who will I meet?
A pearly, white polar bear,
Crunching snow with her feet.

I'm walking through the bushlands.
What will I find?
A funny, hairy baboon,
With a bright, red behind.

So many places to visit,
So many creatures to see.
Mother Nature is amazing,
Animals roaming wild and free.

Frank

I won a goldfish at the fayre,
But my mother went spare.
We didn't have a tank,
For my new friend Frank.

I put him in an old tub,
That would be his little hub.
'Til he got his new home,
Where he could roam.

I went out to the shops,
To buy pebbles and props.
A fancy treasure chest,
And a cave for him to nest.

He looked pretty happy,
Swam around quite snappy.
Between the green reeds,
He has all that he needs.

I checked him in the morning,
I was tired and yawning.
When I heard a voice, I'm sure,
From the tank's rocky floor.

I looked straight at my fish,
And watched his tail swish.
I saw his mouth bobbing,
He looked like he was sobbing.

I gave him some food,
'There you go little dude.'
On the flakes he dined,
'I'm still hungry.' he whined.

I couldn't believe my ears,
I almost cried happy tears.
I did nothing but gawk,
My fish Frank can talk!

Bath Time

A bathtub filled with water,
Is as plain as it can be.
I'd like a bath filled with ice cream,
With a flake as tall as me.

A bathtub filled with water,
Is as boring as it gets.
I'd like a bath filled with cake,
And chocolate loaded jets.

A bathtub filled with water,
Is nothing special at all.
I'd like a bath filled with jelly,
And a peanut butter haul.

A bathtub filled with water,
The same thing every day.
I'd like a bath filled with hot cocoa,
With a candy cane sleigh.

A bathtub filled with water,
That's just not very fun.
I'd like a bath filled with sand,
So I can bathe in the sun.

A bathtub filled with water,
It really makes me snooze.
I'd like a bath filled with popcorn,
What flavour would I choose?

A bathtub filled with water,
It sounds so very dull.
I'd like a bath filled with gumdrops,
I'm sure I'd never get full.

A bathtub filled with water,
Pointless to the brim.
I'd like a bath filled with slime,
So I could try to swim.

A bathtub filled with water,
I could make it less bland.
I'll add lots of soapy bubbles,
And a bath bomb would be grand.

What's Behind the Big, Oak Door?

What's behind the big, oak door?
Wherever will it lead?
Perhaps to an enchanted land,
With a knight and his noble steed.

What's behind the big, oak door?
Wherever will it go?
Maybe to the great North Pole,
Covered in sparkling snow.

What's behind the big, oak door?
I wonder what it could be?
I might see a swaying pirate ship,
Travelling the deep, blue sea.

What's behind the big, oak door?
Could it go anywhere?
Cotton candy, popcorn and more,
At a wondrous, magical fair.

What's behind the big, oak door?
I wonder, which place?

Maybe I'll meet an alien,
Travelling through outer space.

What's behind the big, oak door?
Should I open it to see?
If it takes me to a circus,
Will you travel there with me?

What's behind the big, oak door?
The possibilities never end.
A million places to visit,
My imagination is my friend.

Who's Duck is This?

Who's duck is this? I just don't know,
I found it in my garden though.
Next to where the roses grow,
It tried to nibble on my big toe.

Who's duck is this? My toe, it aches,
I wonder if it's Mr. Drake's.
He owns the bakery by the lakes,
And makes the most delicious cakes.

Who's duck is this? I lick my lips,
They're covered in sticky, icing drips.
Perhaps Miss. Fisher has some tips,
She sells yummy fish and chips.

Who's duck is this? It sure does eat,
I throw a chip down at its feet.
I follow the snicket down the street,
To Mr. Boo's shop, Trick or Treat.

Who's duck is this? How'd it escape?
I love my new, black vampire cape.

I head on over to Get In Shape,
Miss. Jump says nothing, her mouth agape.

Who's duck is this? I skip and hop,
I can't give up, I must not stop.
Suddenly, I have an idea that's top,
Mr. Bobby will know, he's a cop!

Who's duck is this? I must search quicker,
Mr. Bobby gave me a bravery sticker.
I pass the church and see a flicker,
Mr. Rev is there, he's our new vicar.

Who's duck is this? Nobody knows,
I blow out the candle as it glows.
I head back home full of woes,
How did it end up by the rose?

Who's duck is this? I'm feeling glum,
I pluck a rose and prick my thumb.
'Ducky please, where are you from?'
'It's your new pet.' replies my mum.

Who's duck is this? 'It's mine, you say?'
'Of course it is, Happy Birthday!'.
Who's duck is this? I can't wait to play.
It's mine, it's mine! Quack quack hooray.

Sometimes I Have a Worry

Sometimes I have a worry,
That grows in my belly.
Sometimes it gets so big,
That it turns my knees to jelly.

My worry makes me really sad,
And often quite alone.
It follows me everywhere,
I can't leave it at home.

I don't want to think about it,
But when I do, I cry.
I would like for it to go away,
What else can I try?

My worry has grown bigger,
I feel like I might burst.
How do I get it out of me?
Should I tell someone first?

I go and find my Mummy,
To tell her about my worry.

I take my time explaining,
There's no need to hurry.

She kisses away my tears,
And gives me a big hug.
She says if you share a problem,
It gets rid of the worry bug.

I put my hand over my tummy,
My worry is shrinking.
I should have told sooner,
What was I thinking?

Now whenever I get a worry,
I have nothing to fear.
I just tell someone I trust,
To make it disappear.

My Class

The kids in my class are a hoot,
One boy there is called Brute.
He eats beans for dinner,
Says they're a winner,
Then he does nothing but toot.

There's also a girl called Heather,
Who's incredibly clever.
She loves taking a test,
She thinks she's the best,
She fails them almost never.

There's another girl called Rose,
Who always picks her nose.
She doesn't care if she's seen,
She'll pull out a big green,
Then wipe it right on her clothes.

The silliest boy there is Ben,
Don't ever lend him your pen.
He'll chew on the end,
His dad won't be his friend,
He's got ink on his shirt again.

There's also a girl called Sue,

Who always needs the loo.
Please Miss, I can't wait,
Please Miss, it'll be too late,
She'll never learn, it's true.

My best friend there is Matt,
He liked to wear his top hat.
Until one day he sat down,
Turned his smile to a frown,
He'd squashed his top hat - splat.

Matt's twin sister is Mary,
She believes she's a fairy.
She wears purple wings,
Swishes her wand and sings,
When she does spells she's scary.

The tallest boy is called Fred,
He always bangs his head.
At least twice a day,
He knocks it I'd say,
It must be made out of lead.

There's a boy called Owen,
His favourite sport is rowing.
He might go in with a splash,
Or even have a crash,
If he doesn't look where he's going.

Birthday

B is for birthday - it comes once a year,

I is for ice cream that fills me with cheer.

R is for ribbons, wrapped around balloons,

T is for tasty treats and watching cartoons.

H is for hat - a special birthday one,

D is for dressing up, having lots of fun.

A is for amazing, my friends have been to play,

Y is for yawning - it's the end of a super day.

Give Me a Pizza That!

In the middle of a dark, winding wood,
A very hungry and curious, little boy stood.

At the sight before him, his mouth fell open
wide,
He started to drool, have his blue eyes just lied?

Straight ahead and through the giant trees,
He spied a roof made entirely of cheese!

The rooftop was covered with toppings galore,
Pepperoni, peppers, tomatoes and more.

All four walls were stuffed to the crust,
Should he taste it? Oh yes, he must!

He tiptoed forwards, now he was close,
A smell of garlic filled up his nose.

He wondered if it would be quite impolite,
If he was to take just a tiny bite?

Not the whole house, that's for sure,
Perhaps just a window or even the door?

His empty belly growled and grumbled,
As he rushed forwards, he tripped and stumbled.

Gazing up at the grease filled gutters,
'Is this even real?' the little boy mutters.

He stopped just short of the scrumptious dough,
Not wanting to be hasty, taking it slow.

He wanted to savour each and every bite,
Of the mouth watering, pizza house delight.

Reaching out with his trembling hand,
He heard a deep voice roar a strange command.

'Before you take a step, I must be heard,
You must promise me this and give me your
word!'

'You'll take only one bite, and then you must
leave,
Don't you dare try to trick me, lie or deceive.'

'If you are tempted to have even one extra lick,
Let this be your warning, you will surely get
sick.'

The boy looked around, first left and then right,
There was nobody near, no creature in sight.

'I must have imagined it.' the little boy said,
He shrugged his shoulders and went right ahead.

He stuffed his face, ignoring the advice,
Filling his belly with slice after slice.

He gobbled stringy, mozzarella bricks,
And nibbled on crunchy, herby breadsticks.

He devoured sweet pineapple and thinly sliced
ham,
And pulled a face at the green olive doorjamb.

All of a sudden, he started to feel weird,
Once most of the pizza dough had disappeared.

His full, gurgling tummy started to swell,
He slumped down on the floor, he didn't feel
well.

He had indigestion, he'd been far too speedy,
He definitely shouldn't have been so greedy.

A loud, scary voice bellowed in the night,
'I warned you, dear boy, just to take one bite!'

'I'm so very sorry, why didn't I listen?'
The boy's eyes teared up and started to glisten.

'Your apology, to me, seems honest and real,
So, just this once, I will help you to heal.'

He gazed up to the dark sky with amazement
and wonder,
Enchanted by the sounds of a magical thunder.

The clouds opened up, rain started to drizzle,
The house began to melt, droop down and fizzle.

The colours all around him began to fade,
The trees soon vanished, making him afraid.

From far away, he heard his mother calling,
The muddy floor broke open, soon he was
falling.

With a swoosh through the air and a soft, fluffy
landing,
He looked around and on his bed he was
standing.

The pizza house was no more, gone without a
trace.
All that was left was a chewed up pillowcase.

The Farmyard

There once was a cow named Sally,
Who decided to take up ballet.
She tripped on her udder,
Fell down with a judder,
And rolled back home to the valley.

There once was a pig called Spike,
Who wanted to ride a bike.
He went down with a shout,
As he fell on his snout,
And decided instead he'd hike.

There once was a goose named Gretel,
Who's favourite music was metal.
She danced through the moor,
Until her feet were sore,
Then went home to put on the kettle.

There once was a horse named Wayne,
Who hated wearing his rein.
Until one day he coughed,
And his jockey fell off,
And got tangled up in his mane.

There once was a duck called Jack,

Who forgot to wear his mac.
He fell into a puddle,
And got all in a muddle,
So went home to wash his back.

There once was a goat called Drew,
Who longed to visit the zoo.
She dreamed of it all night,
And woke up with a fright,
When she heard a cock-a-doodle-doo.
There once was a cow named Sally,
Who decided to take up ballet.
She tripped on her udder,
Fell down with a judder,
And rolled back home to the valley.

There once was a pig called Spike,
Who wanted to ride a bike.
He went down with a shout,
As he fell on his snout,
And decided instead he'd hike.

There once was a goose named Gretel,
Who's favourite music was metal.
She danced through the moor,
Until her feet were sore,
Then went home to put on the kettle.

There once was a horse named Wayne,

Who hated wearing his rein.
Until one day he coughed,
And his jockey fell off,
And got tangled up in his mane.

There once was a duck called Jack,
Who forgot to wear his mac.
He fell into a puddle,
And got all in a muddle,
So went home to wash his back.

There once was a goat called Drew,
Who longed to visit the zoo.
She dreamed of it all night,
And woke up with a fright,
When she heard a cock-a-doodle-doo.

My Teacher is a Witch

My teacher is a witch,
I'm sure that she must be.
She cackles when she laughs,
And drinks strange, herbal tea.

My teacher is a witch,
I'm positive it's true.
She has a long, pointy nose,
And a black cat that likes to mew.

My teacher is a witch,
There's no place for her to hide.
She carries old, thick books,
And I'm sure there's spells inside.

My teacher is a witch,
I swear it's not a lie.
There's a broomstick in the cupboard,
Although I've never seen her fly.

My teacher is a witch,
I wonder if she has a wand.

Or a cauldron full of potions,
And speckled frogs in her pond.

My teacher is a witch,
But she really is the best.
Perhaps I could be one too,
If she put me to the test.

My teacher is a witch,
A secret in my school.
My teacher is a witch,
I think it's pretty cool!

Child of Mine

C is for child of mine - you are funny, brave and bright,

H is for holding me captive, with your fierce, sparkling light.

I is for impossible to forget - the magical day you were born,

L is for little fingers and toes, my love for you sworn.

D is for don't ever forget how amazing you truly are,

R is for right from the start, you were a super, shining star.

E is for everyone would love to have a friend just like you,

N is for never give up, be kind, work hard and be true.

My Very Best Friend

Having a very best friend,
Is a feeling like no other.
They mean as much to me,
As a sister or a brother.

They come over to my house,
To play lots of silly games.
We're always kind to each other,
Never call anyone names.

We laugh at the same things,
And we share all of our toys.
Mum sometimes shouts upstairs,
Please don't make too much noise.

We tell our favourite stories,
And eat our favourite snacks.
We watch our favourite movie,
And get comfy and relax.

I sometimes get upset,
When it's time for them to go.

But I know I'll see them soon,
Time will fly by, I know.

Our friendship grows each day,
From the start to the end.
It's a feeling like no other,
Having a very best friend.

The Strangest Pirate Ship

When I climbed aboard the pirate ship,
I noticed something strange.
The oars were made from candy canes,
The treasure was chocolate change.

I stomped on the honeycomb decking,
Took hold of the liquorice netting.
Looked across the sugary vessel,
And noticed the pirates fretting.

'What's wrong?' I asked the first mate,
'We're in trouble.' he replied with a sniff.
'The gingerbread wheel's too stiff to turn,
If we're not careful, we'll hit the cliff!'

I saw the dangerous crags looming,
And looked around for an idea.
The rice paper flags were billowing,
The Captain's face was full of fear.

I need to loosen the wheel I thought,
Grabbing the first thing I found.

I launched a bucket of frosty icing,
All over the wheel and ground.

I took hold of the wheel and tugged hard,
But it just didn't want to budge.
I tried another bucket from nearby,
This time filled with melted fudge.

The wheel was getting quite sticky,
Vanilla frosting only made things worse.
My last hope was treacle sauce,
The Captain declared it was a curse.

The jagged cliffs were getting closer,
We almost became a shark's meal.
When a lightbulb pinged over my head,
We needed to build a new wheel.

'Everyone, quickly come here!' I hollered,
Breaking pieces of the wheel off to share.
'Eat it as fast as you can.' I urged,
'I have a plan to end this nightmare.'

I gathered up biscuits and candies,
And used caramel for the glue.
Until I had something similar,
To the wheel I told everyone to chew.

I hoped that it would hold together,

There wasn't much time to waste.
I stuck it onto the peppermint stick,
And swizzled it around in haste.

I looked at the crew in amazement,
My invention was turning the boat.
The Captain stood up and gave cheers,
Away from danger, we began to float.

'You've saved my ship and my crew!"
The Captain exclaimed with glee.
'If it wasn't for your quick thinking,
We'd surely be at the bottom of the sea.'

'However can we repay you?' he asked,
'Maybe a job - you'd come in handy.'
'I have to get home.' I replied with thanks,
But could I take some cotton candy?

Hallow's Eve

H is for Halloween, spooky but delicious,

A is for awesome costumes, scary and fictitious.

L is for lots of sweets in my pumpkin bag,

L is for look out - don't bump into the hag.

O is for October, the 31st really rocks,

W is for witches, werewolves and warlocks.

S is for seriously scary, squeals and screams,

E is for eerie, don't end up with bad dreams.

V is for vampires who hate the bright sunlight,

E is for empty bowls, it's time to call it a night.

Snappy Visits the Dentist

My best friend is a crocodile,
He eats too many sweets.
He chomps buckets full of popcorn,
And takes up four cinema seats.

He doesn't use his toothbrush,
His breath is rather smelly.
He eats giant bags of crisps,
And munches watching telly.

One day he came into school.
With an ice pack on his jaw.
I asked him what was wrong,
He said his tooth was sore.

'Have you brushed them?' I asked,
'Your teeth are likely rotten.'
He blushed and looked at the floor,
And said he had forgotten.

'You need to see a dentist.'
I said to my friend Snappy.

He said he was too scared to go,
He didn't look very happy.

I told him not to be afraid,
He cried some crocodile tears.
I told him not to worry,
And put to rest his fears.

As he laid in the dentist's chair,
He put up quite the fight.
When he was told to open wide,
He snapped his mouth shut tight.

The dentist jumped up from his seat,
He'd almost lost a thumb!
Snappy apologised right away,
And said 'Are we almost done?'

The dentist said 'Let's try again.'
This time Snappy let him look.
He used his tiny mirror,
Then took out a special book.

Inside was filled with stickers,
Snappy chose a bright, red truck.
The dentist found the problem,
A piece of food had gotten stuck.

Snappy grinned, the pain was gone,

He was no longer cross.
He promised to look after his teeth,
And wouldn't forget to floss.

My best friend is a crocodile,
He brushes his teeth day and night.
He doesn't chomp so many sweets,
Now his teeth are sparkly and white.

Hurry Up! Slow Down!

'Hurry up Mum! I don't want to be late,
What if they've already locked the gate?
I didn't take too long getting dressed at all,
I got out straight out of bed when I heard you
call.'

'Hurry up Dad! My teacher might be cross,
I brushed my teeth and used a strand of floss.
I ate all my breakfast in just a few bites,
I made my bed and I switched off all the lights.'

'Hurry up sister! Time is passing on,
By the time we're there, the morning will be
gone.
I made sure my face was washed very well,
I didn't chat back once and I didn't even yell.'

'Hurry up brother! We need to walk out the
door,
We need to go now, I can't take it anymore.
I've wrapped up warm in my scarf, gloves and
hat,

I've been sitting here for hours on the door mat.'

'Wait a minute Polly.' my Mum says,
'It took some time to wake you from your
snoozy daze.'
'Wait a minute Polly.' my Dad calls to the door,
'Your pillows are all over the messy bedroom
floor.'

'Wait a minute Polly.' my sister shouts,
'There's water everywhere, you didn't turn off
the spouts.'
'Wait a minute Polly.' my brother cries,
'Your coat's inside out and your hat's over your
eyes.'

'Slow down Polly.' my family all say,
'You rushed too many things at the start of the
day.'
Slow down Polly, I'll tell myself tonight,
I promise that tomorrow I will try to get it right.

The Tooth Fairy

My tooth, my tooth! It's finally out,
I want to dance and sing and shout.

It's been rather wobbly for a while,
Now I have a huge gap in my smile.

I want a coin that's shiny and bright,
When the tooth fairy visits tonight.

I'll put it under my pillow right now,
I've brushed every day, kept my vow.

Tonight's the night - I will be ready,
I'll be quiet, keep my nerves steady.

Eyes wide open, I'll have a keen ear,
I hope to catch the tooth fairy this year.

Christmas

C is for Christmas - a day that's full of joy,

H is for hopeful that I get a brand new toy.

R is for Rudolph with his red, shiny nose,

I is for imagine if this year it actually snows!

S is for Santa, please don't get stuck in my chimney,

T is for tinsel, wrapped around the Christmas tree.

M is for merry, with all my family and friends,

A is for all together - I hope this day never ends.

S is for stuffing our tummies with yummy food,

D is for dancing - we're in the holiday mood.

A is for amazing, all I've done is smile,

Y is for Yule log, let's finish this day in style!

Months of the Year

January brings with it the cold and snow,
Making our fingers freeze and noses glow.

February brings to us Saint Valentine,
Sharing our love, yours and mine.

March brings the beginning of Spring,
Lambs are born and we hear birds sing.

April brings sunshine and drizzly showers,
The ground is scattered in beautiful flowers.

May brings cheerful music and soul,
Dancers twirl around the ribboned maypole.

June brings Summer and glorious sun,
The rain goes away and we can have fun.

July brings the end of the school year,
No more work to do, all the children cheer.

August brings hot days and cooling ice cream,
Swimming costumes on, paddling in the stream.

September brings crispy leaves on the ground,

Autumn has begun, falling conkers to be found.

October brings spooky pumpkins and frights,
The clocks turn back - shorter days, longer
nights.

November brings dazzling firework shows,
Toffee apples are eaten, hot chocolate flows.

December brings Santa and his little elves,
Christmas trees are trimmed, mince pies on the
shelves.

The year soon ends - what will the next one have
in store?
Celebrations end, time to start January again
once more.

ABOUT THE AUTHOR

43

Rachel Bishop was born in Sheffield, England in 1992. When she isn't fumbling her way through raising two young humans, she's an avid reader. This book is her first and, so far, her best book of poetry.